PRIVILEGES OF THE ABBOT OF CANTERBURY

St. Augustine of Canterbury

Archbishop of Canterbury

Translated by: D.P. Curtin

Dalcassian
Publishing
Company

PHILADELPHIA, PA

ISBN: 978-1-960069-84-9 (Paperback)

Library of Congress Control Number:
Author: Curtin, D.P. (1985-)

Printed by Ingram Content Group, 1 Ingram Blvd, La Vergne, Tennessee

First printing edition 2017.

Introduction

Like many documents that are associated with King Aethelbert and St. Augustine of Canterbury, this one is of questionable authenticity. It lays out the familiar claim that the Monastery of Sts. Peter and Paul is permanently under the jurisdiction of the Roman Catholic Church and proprietarily cannot be separated from the See of Rome. As a point of English law, similar guarantees are made in both Magna Carta and in the king's own coronation oath. However, the author of this text appears to "protest too much", granting little information about the nature of the charter, its parameters, or the detailed context of such a conclave. Instead, the emphasis is placed on its relationship to Rome and the immunity of the church from any temporal power. Suspiciously, this appears to be a work of the 16th century, when the abbey-church was dissolved by King Henry VIII in 1538. Anglo-Catholics who were, then as now, appalled by the royal encroach into church property saw this as an act of theft, if not outright blasphemy.

Historically, the ruins of the abbey still stand, and the bishopric of Canterbury remains, albeit as part of the Church of England. Its grounds were used for monastic education for almost a thousand years prior to the edict of the Tudor king. It is hard to translate the cataclysm of the destruction of a thousand-year-old library into comprehension for a modern audience. The collected knowledge of all of English history was retained by the church, as the great custodian of English culture, and held in continuity with the passing of centuries and dynastic families. The presence of the church in England remained as the only source of continuity that the common people were familiar with, following the various waves of invasions: Saxons, Jutes, Angles, Danes, Norman, French, Scots, et cetera. For that reason, the abbey is a fitting legacy for King Henry VIII, or more accurately a perfect symbol of his reign:

the labor of centuries destroyed in an instant by the whim of a fat, lecherous oaf.

In the 19th century, the Church of England sought to revive some of their ancient traditions as best possible, with the restoration of some monastic orders within the church. This included a renewed interest in the site of the abbey at Canterbury, recently renamed St. Augustine's Abbey. It has been partially restored to its educational function via The King's School. However, the wealth of knowledge has been lost, including any additional writings by the historical St. Augustine of Canterbury. Perhaps the recent sharp decline in attendance to the Church of England will force a realignment of the church to its historic roots in Western Christianity. Or, conversely, it might double down on the anomie that so many protestant churches have endorsed in our current century and continue down the short road to extinction.

D.P. Curtin
August 3, 2017
Wexford, PA

Augustine, the bishop of Dorobernia, a servant of the see, whom the most blessed Pope Gregory, inspired by divine clemency, sent as legate to procure the English nation to God. To all his successors, the bishops, and to all the kings of England with their posterity, and to all the faithful of God, and in faith and grace, peace and safety.

It is clear to all that King Athelbertus, beloved of God, the first of the English kings consecrated to the kingdom of Christ, at our insistence and his prodigal benevolence among the other churches he made and bishoprics, royally founded a monastery outside his metropolis, Dorobernia, in honor of the princes of the apostles Peter and Paul and with royal resources and he enriched and magnified it with large possessions, and with perpetual liberty, and fortified the kingdom with every right, with all things and judgments, within and without, pertaining to it. I, too, the helper and patron of the same freedom, all my successors, archbishops, and all ecclesiastical or secular powers, through the Lord Jesus Christ and his apostles, object to the reverence, and I forbid, by the apostolic injunction of our mentioned Father, that no one shall ever have any power, or dominion, or governance over the sabbath, or he presumes to usurp the apostolic monastery, or the lands, or the churches belonging to it, and he does not disturb or oppress the ministers of God under any conditions of subjugation, servitude, or tribute, either in great or in the smallest degree.

An abbot elected by his brothers in the same monastery should not be ordained to his service, but to the Sunday service, and should not obey him but advise God. Indeed, he does not regard him as a subject, but as a brother, or as a consort, but as a colleague, and as a minister in the Sunday work. He does not perform mass there as if at the altar of his dominion, nor perform ordinations or benedictions usurpably without the request of the abbot or of the brothers.

Of the devil, who fell from heaven by the tyranny of pride. The kings of the nations (says the Lord) rule over them, but not so over you. And when tribute is received from strangers and not from the children, so the Lord himself concludes, therefore the children are free. With this irreverence, therefore, do the fathers of the churches claim dominion over the children of the kingdom of God, and above all over this Church, the treasury of the saints, in whose mother's womb we hope the bodies of so many priests, kings, and princes of Dorobernia will be reburied in peace, by apostolic authority, and resurrected from here to eternal glory.

If any one, not fearing to offend such friends of the supreme judge, violates the statutes of this privilege, or imitates the violator and holds his power, let him know that he will be punished by the apostolic sword of the blessed Peter through his vicar, Gregory, unless he makes amends.

Therefore, all of these things as they are here, written with the apostolic verification and authority of our founder Gregory himself, we have been sanctioned by, and confirmed by his own mouth, in the presence of the glorious king Athelbert with his son Ethelbald, and all the royal nobles who join him in praise. In turn this took place with our most reverend brothers from the holy Church of Rome who were destined to come here with me or for me in the gospel of the Lord, namely, Lawrence, whom we have appointed as our successor, by the favor of God, and Mellitus bishop of London, and Justus bishop of Rofensi, and Peter the venerable, the first abbot of the princes of the apostles of the same monastery, with the rest helpers in the Lord by pressing my demands, and at the same time exercising a blessing on those who have faithfully kept these things, or on those who repent, which we do not want on the transgressors.

LATIN TEXT

Privilegium abbatiae Cantuariensis

Augustinus, episcopus Doroberniae sedis famulus, quem superna inspirante clementia, beatissimus papa Gregorius Anglicae genti Deo acquirendae legatarium misit amministrum; omnibus successoribus suis episcopis, cunctisque Angliae regibus cum suis posteris atque omnibus Dei fidelibus et in fide et gratia pacem et salutem. Patet omnibus quod Deo amabilis rex Athelbertus, primus Anglorum regum Christi regno sacratus, nostra instantia et sua prodiga benevolentia inter caeteras ecclesias quas fecit et episcopia, monasterium extra metropolim suam Doroberniam, in honore principum apostolorum Petri et Pauli regaliter condidit et regalibus opibus amplisque possessionibus ditavit, magnificavit, perpetuaque libertate, et omni iure regio cum omnibus rebus et iudiciis, intus et foris illi pertinentibus, munivit, suoque regio privilegio et superni iudicii imprecatione, atque apostolica sancti papae Gregorii interminatione excommunicatoria, contra omnem iniuriam confirmavit. Ego quoque eiusdem libertatis adiutor et patrocinator omnes successores meos archiepiscopos, omnesque ecclesiasticas vel saeculares potestates per Dominum Iesum Christum et apostolorum eius reverentiam obtestor, atque apostolica memorati Patris nostri interminatione interdico, ne quisquam unquam ullum potentatum, aut dominatum, aut imperium in hoc dominicum vel apostolicum monasterium, vel terras, vel ecclesias ad illud pertinentes usurpare praesumat, nec ulla prorsus subiugationis aut servitutis, aut tributi conditione, vel in magno, vel in minimo, Dei ministros inquietet aut opprimat. (Abbatem a suis fratribus electum in eodem monasterio non ad suum famulatum, sed ad dominicum ministerium ordinet, nec sibi hunc obaudire sed Deo suadeat; nec vero sibi subiectum, sed fratrem, sed consortem, sed collegam, et coministrum in opus dominicum eum reputet. Non ibi missas quasi ad suae ditionis altare nec ordinationes vel benedictiones usurpative sine abbatis, vel fratrum petitione exerceat, nullum sibi ius consuetudinarium vel in vilissima re exigat quatenus pacis concordia unum sint in dominio utrinque, nec quisquam, quod absit, dominandi dissidio in iudicium incidat diaboli, qui superbiae tyrannide corruit de coelo. Reges gentium (inquit Dominus) dominatur eorum, vos autem non sic. Cumque ab alienis non a filiis accipiantur tributa, sic ipse Dominus concludit, ergo liberi sunt filii. Qua ergo irreverentia Patres ecclesiarum in filios regni Dei sibi vindicant dominationem, maxime autem in hanc Ecclesiam sanctorum thesaurarium, in cuius materno utero tot pontificum Doroberniae regumque ac principum corpora speramus alma refovenda sepulturae requie, ex auctoritate scilicet apostolica, et hinc ad aeternam gloriam resuscitanda. Tales supremi iudicis amicos si quis offendere non metuens huius privilegii statuta violaverit, vel violatorem imitando vim suam tenuerit, sciat se apostolico beati Petri gladio iper suum vicarium Gregorium puniendum nisi emendaverit. Haec ergo omnia, uti hic sunt, scripta, apostolica ipsius institutoris nostri Gregorii comprobatione et auctoritate servanda sancimus, suoque ore confirmamus, praesente glorioso rege Athelberto cum filio suo Ethelbaldo, et collaudantibus cum ipso omnibus optimatibus regiis, atque ultro volentibus reverentissimis fratribus nostris a sancta Romae Ecclesiae huc mecum vel ad me in Evangelium Domini destinatis, scilicet Laurentio, quem nobis, Deo favente, successorem constituimus, et Mellito Lundoniae episcopo, et Iusto Rofensi episcopo, et Petro vene abili eiusdem monasterii principum apostolorum abbate primo, cum caeteris in Domino adiutoribus meis obnixe postulantibus, simulque in eos qui haec fideliter servaverint benedictionem, aut in impoenitentes, quod nolumus, transgressores damnationem exercentibus.

The Scriptorium Project is the work of a small group of lay people of various apostolic churches who are interested in the preservation, transmission, and translation of the works of the early and medieval church. Our efforts are to make the works of the church fathers accessible to anyone who might have an interest in Christian antiquities and the theological, philosophical, and moral writings that have become the bedrock of Western Civilization.

To-date, our releases have pulled from the Greek, Syriac, Georgian, Latin, Celtic, Ethiopian, and Coptic traditions of Christianity, and have been pulled from sundry local traditions and languages.

Other Titles and Translations by D.P. Curtin:

Lebor Gabala Erenn by Nennius the Monk (2017)
The Eight Vices by Eutropis of Valencia (2017)
Three Letters from the Companion of the Bulgars by St. Rupert of Juvavum (2017)
Privileges of the Abbot of Canterbury by St. Augustine of Canterbury (2017)
Nicene Canons in the Old Nubian Language (2018)
Apology to Gunthamund, King of Vandals by Aemeilius Dracontius (2018)
First Book of Ethiopian Maccabees (2018)
Chronicon: a short chronicle of Visigothic Spain by Eutrandus of Ticino (2019)
Decrees of Aethelbert by St. Aethelbert, King of Kent (2019)
The Measure to be taxed for Penance by St. Columba of Iona (2019)
Protoevangelium of James: Greek and English Texts (2019)
Edicts of the Synod of Paris by Chlothar II, King of Franks (2019)
The Life of St. Desiderius by Sisebut, King of Visigoths (2019)
The Synod of Rome by St. Boniface IV of Rome (2019)
Letter to Pope Theodore by Victor of Carthage (2020)
The Decree of 610 by Gundemar, King of Visigoths (2020)
Laws of the Church by Chlothar III, King of Franks (2020)
Donations by St. Aethelbert, King of Kent (2020)
The Mystical Interpretation by St. Aileran the Wise (2020)
Laws of the Church by St. Dagobert II, King of Franks (2020)
The Old Nubian Miracle of St. Mena (2021)
About Fifteen Problems by St. Albertus Magnus (2022)
Testament of Some Former Things by John Scotus Eriugena (2022)
The Georgian Synaxarium (2022)
Instructions: Counsel for Novices by St. Ammonas the Hermit (2022)
The Syriac Menologium and Martyrology (2022)
Book on Religious Exercise and Quiet by St. Isaiah the Solitary (2022)
Vision of Theophilus by St. Cyril of Alexandria (2022)
On Fate (De Fato) by St. Albertus Magnus (2023)
Fragments of 'Chronicle' by Hippolytus of Thebes (2023)
Life of the Blessed Theotokos by Epiphanius Monachus (2023)
Syriac Life of John the Baptist by Serapion the Presbyter (2023)
Second Book of Ethiopian Maccabees (2023)